THE UQ AI EFFECT

Intelligent Leadership in a VUCA World

KATIA DORIA FONSECA VASCONCELOS

Dedication:

To my beloved children, Mario (Teik), Bruna, Victor, and Bárbara, who are the inspiration and reason behind my relentless pursuit of knowledge. You are my strength and motivation to share my ideas and experiences.

To my husband José de Vasconcelos Filho, whose collaboration and support were instrumental in creating this book. Your unwavering dedication and support are a precious gift in my life.

To my dear grandchildren, Davi, Vivi, and João Gabriel, who represent the continuity of our stories and the hope for a bright future. May this book inspire you to explore your passions and seek truth in all things.

To my sons-in-law and daughters-in-law, Nikolas Bucvar, Eduardo, Jana, and Jacque, who strengthen our family with their love, support, and valuable contributions.

I am grateful for being part of this journey and for sharing your enriching perspectives and experiences.

This is dedicated to all of you, my beloved family, with all my love and gratitude.

Katia Doria Fonseca Vasconcelos

INTRODUCTION

In the VUCA world, where volatility, uncertainty, complexity, and ambiguity are constant, traditional leadership based on vertical hierarchies is no longer effective in addressing the challenges and uncertainties that permeate the business environment. Organizations need to adopt a new leadership approach that is agile, adaptable, and collaborative.

In this context, the concept of the UQ AI effect emerges, representing the powerful combination of Universal Synchronic Intelligence Quotient (UQ) and the strategic application of Artificial Intelligence (AI). This innovative approach aims to balance human potential with technological support, transforming leadership into a stabilizing force amidst chaos.

The UQ AI effect functions like the flapping of a butterfly's wings, triggering a series of events and causing a cascading effect. Similarly, intelligent leadership based on the UQ AI effect has the power to positively influence the course of events, directing the transformation from VUCA to a new era of stability and success.

By balancing human potential represented by UQ with the strategic application of AI, it is possible to create a collaborative, committed, and productive work environment. Leadership shifts from being vertical to shared, valuing collaboration and synergy among team members. This approach allows everyone to have the opportunity to contribute and influence outcomes, enhancing individual skills for the collective benefit.

The strategic application of AI in intelligent leadership brings significant benefits by facilitating communication, optimizing processes, and providing decision-making support. AI technologies can be used to share information, analyze data, and identify patterns, contributing to well-informed and efficient decision-making.

By adopting the UQ AI effect in leadership in a VUCA world, organizations will be better prepared to face challenges with confidence, adaptability, and efficiency. Shared and collaborative leadership, combined with the strategic use of AI, drives the creation of a more innovative, resilient, and productive work environment.

In this book, we will delve deep into the power of the UQ AI effect in intelligent leadership in a VUCA world. We will analyze case studies, scientific research, and relevant theories to provide a comprehensive and evidence-based insight into how to harness the butterfly effect of UQ AI to positively influence the transformation of VUCA. Throughout the following pages, you will discover how this concept can catalyze change and drive stability and success in your organization.

We hope to pique your interest and invite you to embark on this journey of discovery and transformation. Let's explore together the power of the UQ AI effect and its application in intelligent leadership in an ever-changing world.

INITIAL CONSIDERATIONS

In the VUCA world, traditional vertical leadership no longer proves effective in facing the challenges and uncertainties that permeate the business environment. For organizations to thrive in this constantly evolving scenario, it is crucial to adopt a new leadership approach. In this context, leaders must prepare for a new way of assigning their roles, where collaboration and synergy among team members are valued.

By implementing the concept of UQ throughout the team, extraordinary results can be achieved. UQ acts as a driving force that stimulates collaboration, commitment, and productivity among team members. Through the calibration of UQ in each individual, we create an environment conducive to creativity, innovation, and the resolution of complex problems.

In this new form of leadership, the focus shifts from the figure of the leader at the top of the hierarchy to the team as a whole. Roles are assigned based on individual competencies, and teamwork becomes a priority. Leadership transitions from being vertical to shared, where everyone has the opportunity to contribute and influence outcomes.

Collaboration becomes the foundation for decision-making, enabling the integration of different perspectives and maximizing the potential of each team member. The synergy generated by the calibration of UQ results in a more harmonious work dynamic, where individual talents complement and strengthen each other.

Furthermore, the calibration of UQ fosters a more positive and motivating work environment. Team members feel more engaged, knowing that their contributions are valued and that they are part of something greater. This connection among individuals promotes a sense of belonging and purpose, driving productivity and the achievement of organizational goals.

Therefore, it is imperative for leaders to be prepared for this new way of assigning roles, where collaborative leadership and the calibration of UQ are essential. By adopting this approach, organizations will be better positioned to address the volatility, uncertainty, complexity, and ambiguity of the VUCA world. Collaboration and the balance of UQ become the key to a more collaborative, committed, and productive team, ready to face challenges and achieve exceptional results.

The transition to shared and collaborative leadership is not a simple task. While the traditional hierarchical model is deeply ingrained in business practices, adopting a more horizontal leadership approach requires cultural and structural transformation throughout the organization. Leadership at all levels, from the top hierarchy to the lower levels, needs to align with this new era of sharing.

In this new approach, the concept of UQ (Universal Synchronic Intelligence Quotient) and the tools it provides play a fundamental role. UQ offers a framework that helps develop the necessary skills for shared leadership, such as active listening, clear and transparent communication, and the encouragement of active participation from all team members. Through the balance of UQ, leaders are empowered to make more informed decisions, considering different perspectives and maximizing each individual's potential.

Moreover, AI (Artificial Intelligence) fits perfectly within this type of collaborative management. AI technologies can play a crucial role in facilitating communication, sharing information, and supporting decision-making. For instance, chatbots can be used to provide immediate support and address team members' questions, allowing leaders to focus on strategic tasks and the development of their subordinates' skills. AI algorithms can also assist in data analysis and pattern identification, contributing to a more informed and efficient decision-making process.

However, it is important to highlight that implementing shared leadership and using AI present significant organizational challenges. The shift in mindset and the breaking of paradigms may encounter resistance from established leaders who may feel threatened by the loss of power and control. Therefore, a careful process of awareness, training, and engagement of all organization members, from leaders to collaborators, is necessary to foster a common understanding of the benefits of this approach.

Furthermore, shared leadership requires an open and inclusive organizational culture where the voices of everyone are heard and valued. This entails creating spaces for dialogue, promoting diversity, and appreciating individual contributions. Mutual trust between leaders and subordinates also becomes essential for the success of this model, enabling shared responsibilities and joint decision-making.

By adopting shared leadership and leveraging the tools provided by the UQ concept, combined with the potential of AI, organizations will be better prepared to face the challenges of the present time. The ability to adapt quickly, innovate, and make informed decisions becomes a significant competitive advantage. Shared leadership, coupled with technology, enables the creation of a more collaborative, committed, and productive work environment, driving the overall success of the organization.

We hope that you have understood the importance and potential of the

UQ AI effect in intelligent leadership in a VUCA world. Throughout this book, we will delve deeper into these concepts, providing practical examples, insights, and guidance for you to apply them in your own leadership journey. We are ready to explore together the power of the UQ AI effect and transform VUCA into an era of stability and success.

TABLE OF CONTENTS

UNDERSTANDING THE PRINCIPLES OF UQ

Human success is driven by the balance of the principles of UQ (Universal Synchronic Intelligence Quotient), a concept supported by scientific research and case studies. Several experts and researchers have explored the aspects of UQ and its impact on different areas of human life, providing valuable insights into how to effectively apply these principles.

A study conducted by researchers from Stanford University revealed the importance of developing resilience and emotional control in achieving positive outcomes in careers and relationships. This research highlighted how the ability to cope with adversity and control emotions contributes to making sound decisions and building healthy and productive relationships.

Renowned Harvard Business School professor Clayton Christensen emphasized that disruptive innovation requires a shift in approach and overcoming outdated paradigms. He emphasized that success lies in embracing change and quickly adapting to new circumstances.

Psychologist and Nobel laureate economist Daniel Kahneman reminds us that our decisions are influenced by how we frame problems. By adopting a positive perspective and viewing challenges as learning opportunities, we can make more accurate decisions and achieve superior results. The theory of emotional intelligence, developed by Daniel Goleman, also aligns with the concept of UQ, emphasizing the importance of emotional balance for personal and professional success.

Renowned psychologist and Harvard Graduate School of Education professor Howard Gardner highlights the importance of balancing and developing all of our intelligences. He encourages us to reprogram our educational approach, valuing not only logical-mathematical intelligence but also emotional, musical, spatial, and other intelligences, allowing us to explore our full potential.

These great names, along with other proponents of innovative thinking, reinforce the importance of adopting a new perspective in the face of problems. By understanding and applying the principles of UQ - 360-degree vision, Resilience, Adaptability, Emotional Control, and Synchronicity - we will be prepared to confidently, creatively, and effectively tackle challenges.

Each of these principles plays a fundamental role in seeking balance and developing our potentials. 360-degree vision involves having a broad and comprehensive perspective of all dimensions of our lives, understanding the interconnections between different areas, and identifying opportunities that others may not perceive.

Resilience empowers us to deal with adversity, overcome obstacles, and quickly recover from challenging situations. Developing resilience means learning from difficult experiences, seeking creative solutions, and continuing to move forward even in the face of difficulties.

Adaptability allows us to adjust and adapt to different circumstances and demands. It is the ability to be flexible, open to change, and willing to experiment with new approaches. Developing adaptability challenges, us to step out of our comfort zone, try new ways of doing things, and adapt to changes in our environment.

Emotional Control is essential for dealing with pressure and stress. By developing emotional control, we can recognize our emotions, manage them effectively, and make rational decisions while maintaining emotional balance in challenging situations.

Synchronicity refers to the harmony and coordination of our actions within the environment we are in. It is the ability to synchronize our tasks, projects, and goals to achieve an efficient and effective workflow.

Developing synchronicity challenges us to organize our activities, set priorities, and find ways to optimize our time and resources.

By understanding these principles and seeking balance among them, we will be better prepared to face the challenges of the business environment and achieve personal and professional success. In the next chapter, we will deepen our understanding of each of these principles and how to apply them practically in our lives.

THE PRINCIPLES OF UQ AND THEIR APPLICATION IN LEADERSHIP

The UQ (Universal Synchronic Intelligence Quotient) approach offers a powerful framework for understanding and balancing human potential. These principles of UQ can be applied in team leadership, enabling leaders to develop more collaborative, productive, and goal-aligned work environments.

The first principle, 360-degree vision, involves having a broad and comprehensive perspective of all dimensions of work and the team. Leaders who apply this principle strive to consider different viewpoints, actively listen to team members, and take their contributions and ideas into account. By valuing diversity of opinions, experiences, and knowledge, leaders can make more informed decisions and create an inclusive and participatory work environment.

Resilience is another essential principle in leadership. Resilient leaders can effectively deal with adversity and overcome obstacles. They serve as models of resilience for the team, demonstrating how to face challenges and learn from experiences. By cultivating resilience within the team, leaders promote a positive mindset in the face of adversity, encouraging innovation and the pursuit of creative solutions.

Adaptability is crucial for leading in a constantly changing environment. Adaptive leaders are flexible and open to new ideas, quickly adjusting to emerging demands and challenges. They encourage experimentation and continuous learning, enabling the team to adapt and evolve alongside market transformations. By promoting adaptability, leaders ensure that the team is prepared to face new challenges and seize opportunities.

Emotional Control plays a crucial role in effective leadership. Leaders who possess emotional control can maintain calm and mental clarity, even in stressful or challenging situations. They demonstrate emotional balance, inspiring confidence in the team and facilitating well-grounded decision-making. By developing emotional control, leaders create a more stable and productive work environment.

Finally, Synchronicity is essential for leading teams efficiently. Synchronized leaders can coordinate team activities and deadlines, ensuring a harmonious and effective workflow. They establish clear goals, define priorities, and promote collaboration among team members. By promoting synchronicity, leaders maximize team efficiency and drive results.

By understanding and applying the principles of UQ in leadership, leaders can develop more balanced, engaged teams capable of tackling the challenges of the constantly evolving business environment. By using the UQ test as a metric to assess the balance and development of potentials, leaders can identify areas for improvement, track progress over time, and provide targeted feedback. This UQ-oriented approach promotes a healthier and more productive work environment, driving the success of the team and the organization as a whole.

To illustrate a UQ test, let's use a challenge model:

PROJECT CHALLENGE

Presentation of challenges related to project planning and execution. Questions and practical exercises to test and develop organizational skills, resource management, and strategic thinking.

In the previous chapter, we discussed the importance of preparing for the challenges presented in this book. Now it's time to put the acquired knowledge into practice and take on the first challenge: the Project Challenge.

The Project Challenge is designed to test your skills in project planning, organization, and execution. By taking on this challenge, you will have the opportunity to apply the principles of UQ - 360-degree vision, Resilience, Adaptability, Emotional Control, and Synchronicity - in a real-world context.

Below, we present a series of questions and practical exercises to assist you in this challenge and develop your project-related skills:

Goal Definition: Start by clearly defining the project's objectives.

What results do you want to achieve? What are the success criteria for the project?

Resource Identification: List all the resources needed for the project, such as people, materials, time, and budget. How can you obtain these resources? What limitations or constraints do you need to consider?

Risk Analysis: Identify potential risks associated with the project. What are the threats that can impact the project's success? How can you mitigate these risks and prepare to deal with them?

Step Planning: Divide the project into steps or phases. What are the main tasks that need to be accomplished in each step? What are the dependencies between tasks? How can you organize and prioritize these steps efficiently?

Responsibility Allocation: Assign clear responsibilities for each project task. Who will be responsible for executing each step? How can you ensure clear and effective communication among team members?

Time Management: Develop a realistic schedule for the project. What are the deadlines for each step? How can you ensure that the project is progressing according to the schedule? What strategies can you use to deal with possible delays?

Monitoring and Evaluation: Establish metrics and indicators to track the project's progress. How will you monitor performance against the established objectives? How will you evaluate the success of the project?

When facing the Project Challenge, remember to apply the principles of UQ in every step. Maintain a 360-degree vision, considering all dimensions of the project. Be resilient in the face of challenges and obstacles that may arise. Be open to adapting to changes and seeking innovative solutions. Maintain emotional control, making rational and effective decisions. And synchronize your actions, ensuring an efficient and coordinated workflow.

Through the questions and practical exercises presented in this chapter, you will have the opportunity to test your organizational skills, resource management, and strategic thinking. By taking on this challenge, you will strengthen your UQ principles and develop your capabilities for success in future projects.

Prepare yourself to put your skills to the test and dive headfirst into the Project Challenge. We are confident that you will be able to face the challenges with confidence, creativity, and effectiveness. Remember, the UQ journey of development and balance is just beginning.

UQ TEST:
After completing the adventure trip planning, it's time to self-assess yourself in relation to the UQ principles. Answer the following questions and mark the option that best describes your approach when making decisions related to the trip:

360-degree vision:

I consider different perspectives when making decisions related to the trip.

a) I don't consider additional perspectives.
b) I consider some additional perspectives.

c) I consider several additional perspectives.
d) I consider a wide range of additional perspectives.

Resilience:

I effectively deal with unexpected events or obstacles that may arise during the trip.

a) I struggle to deal with unexpected events.
b) I can overcome some obstacles.
c) I am resilient in most situations.
d) I am highly resilient and able to handle any obstacle.

Adaptability:

I easily adjust to changes in plans or unexpected circumstances during the trip.

a) I struggle to adapt to changes.
b) I can adapt with some effort.
c) I am flexible and adapt well to changes.
d) I am highly adaptable and easily handle any change.

Emotional Control:

I maintain emotional control in stressful or challenging situations during the trip.

a) I have difficulty maintaining emotional control.
b) I can quickly recover from stressful situations.
c) I have good emotional control in most situations.
d) I am able to handle any situation calmly and with emotional balance.

Synchronicity:

I coordinate my activities and deadlines during the trip to maintain a harmonious workflow.

a) I have difficulty synchronizing my activities.
b) I can maintain a reasonable workflow.
c) My activities are well-coordinated most of the time.
d) I can maintain a harmonious and coordinated workflow in all aspects of the trip.

After answering these questions and assigning a score to each of them, add up the points and evaluate your overall balance in relation to the UQ principles:

a: 0 points
b: 1 point
c: 2 points
d: 3 points
Add up the points and evaluate your overall balance:

0 to 5 points: There are significant opportunities to improve your balance in the UQ principles. Identify specific areas where you can work to strengthen these principles.

6 to 10 points: You are on the right track, but there is still room to enhance your balance in the UQ principles. Continue to focus on and practice these principles in your future adventures.

11 to 15 points: Congratulations, your UQ is 100! You have

demonstrated a high level of balance in the UQ principles in your trip planning. Continue to apply these principles in other areas of your life.

The presented test follows the structure of a UQ test, where questions related to the UQ principles are asked, and scores are assigned to each response. This type of test aims to assess the balance of UQ potentials in a specific context, in this case, decision-making related to an adventure trip.

In the test, UQ principles such as 360-degree vision, Resilience, Adaptability, Emotional Control, and Synchronicity are addressed. Each principle is evaluated through questions that measure the individual's ability to apply these principles in specific situations. By assigning points to the answers, it is possible to obtain an overall score that reflects the balance of UQ potentials.

This type of self-assessment test is a useful tool for individuals to identify areas where they can improve their potentials and develop more effective leadership. By understanding their strengths and areas for improvement in relation to UQ, individuals can work on specific skill development and strive for greater balance in their potentials, enabling more effective and adaptable leadership in the VUCA world.

Based on the example UQ test, leaders can use this methodology to assess the UQ of employees in their teams. By assigning specific goals to each challenge within ongoing projects, the test can be applied to measure employees' performance in relation to UQ principles such as

360-degree vision, Resilience, Adaptability, Emotional Control, and Synchronicity.

Using UQ-parameterized AI, relevant data can be collected on employees' performance and risks analyzed regarding projects. AI can be used to identify patterns, assess the balance of UQ potentials in each employee, and provide valuable insights for decision-making.

This approach provides a broader and more objective view of employees' performance in relation to UQ potentials. Based on the results obtained, leaders can implement personal development strategies, offer specific training to strengthen identified areas for improvement, and foster a work environment that promotes growth and collaboration.

Therefore, the application of UQ in conjunction with parameterized AI offers an innovative approach to gauge employees' performance, identify areas for development, and promote a balance of human potentials for project success and excellent customer service.

MAXIMIZING TEAM POTENTIAL

The Impact of Intelligent Leadership on Team Engagement

Intelligent leadership based on UQ principles has a significant impact on team engagement. By adopting a collaborative and shared approach, leaders promote a work environment where all team members feel valued and have the opportunity to actively contribute to organizational goals.

Intelligent leadership encourages active employee participation by listening to their ideas, opinions, and concerns. Leaders understand the importance of building relationships based on trust and mutual respect, which creates a psychologically safe environment where team members feel encouraged to express their ideas and take risks.

Furthermore, intelligent leadership recognizes and values individual contributions. Leaders understand that each team member possesses unique skills and knowledge and seek to create opportunities for those skills to be utilized to their fullest potential. By recognizing and valuing the potential of each employee, leaders promote engagement, motivation, and a sense of belonging.

DEVELOPING COLLABORATION AND PRODUCTIVITY

Collaboration is a key element of intelligent leadership. Leaders encourage collaboration among team members by creating workspaces that foster idea exchange, cooperation, and knowledge sharing. They recognize that innovative solutions and better outcomes are often achieved through teamwork.

To develop collaboration, leaders employ effective communication strategies, establish open channels for information sharing, and promote transparency within the team. They also create opportunities for interdisciplinary collaboration, encouraging diversity of perspectives and joint problem-solving.

Additionally, intelligent leadership seeks to develop a work environment that promotes productivity. Leaders set clear and realistic goals, provide adequate resources and support for team members to perform their roles efficiently. They also identify and remove potential obstacles and ensure that employees' skills and competencies are properly aligned with assigned tasks and responsibilities.

TRANSFORMATIONAL LEADERSHIP AND UQ PRINCIPLES

Transformational leadership is a leadership style that aligns perfectly with UQ principles. It focuses on inspiring and motivating team members to reach their full potential and grow both personally and professionally.

Transformational leaders are change agents, constantly seeking new ways to improve and innovate. They are visionaries and effectively communicate their vision, inspiring team members to embrace change and commit to organizational goals.

By combining UQ principles with transformational leadership, leaders can create an environment that fosters individual and collective growth. They encourage continuous learning, provide constructive feedback, and promote the development of employees' skills. This approach creates a culture of continuous improvement, where team members feel supported and motivated to constantly seek enhancement.

Conclusion

Developing team potential is essential for organizational success. Intelligent leadership based on UQ principles plays a crucial role in driving engagement, collaboration, and productivity among team members. By adopting a transformational approach, leaders can create a dynamic work environment where everyone feels motivated, valued, and capable of achieving exceptional results.

Collaborative Horizontal Leadership: Enabling Leadership Style through UQ and AI Implementation

Collaborative horizontal leadership is a leadership style that becomes viable through the implementation of UQ with AI. In this chapter, we will explore the concept of this leadership style, its fundamental principles, and the benefits it brings to the organization.

The Concept of Collaborative Horizontal Leadership

Collaborative horizontal leadership is a model that breaks away from traditional vertical hierarchies and seeks the active participation of all team members. In this leadership style, power is distributed among collaborators, and decisions are made collaboratively and in a decentralized manner.

DEFINITION AND FUNDAMENTAL PRINCIPLES

In collaborative horizontal leadership, emphasis is placed on collaboration, open communication, and appreciation of individual contributions. Leaders act as facilitators and promote an inclusive work environment where each team member has the opportunity to express their ideas, opinions, and perspectives.

Some of the fundamental principles of collaborative horizontal leadership include:

- Empowerment: Leaders empower collaborators by granting autonomy and responsibility for decision-making and problem-solving.
- Co-creation: Collaborative leadership encourages co-creation, where collaborators work together to generate innovative and creative solutions.
- Knowledge sharing: Leaders facilitate the sharing of knowledge and experiences among team members, fostering a culture of continuous learning.
- Collaboration and synergy: Collaborative horizontal leadership values collaboration and aims to create synergy among the skills and knowledge of team members.
- Benefits and Advantages for the Organization

The implementation of UQ with AI enables collaborative horizontal leadership and brings a range of benefits and advantages to the organization. Some of them include:

- Increased engagement and motivation: Collaborative horizontal leadership actively involves collaborators, increasing their engagement and motivation. Team members feel valued and have the opportunity to contribute their ideas and skills.
- Enhanced decision-making: The diversity of perspectives and knowledge in collaborative horizontal leadership results in more comprehensive and informed decision-making. Collaboration and knowledge sharing enable the identification of the best solutions.

Greater innovation and creativity: Collaborative horizontal leadership stimulates innovation and creativity by promoting co-creation and collective thinking. The diversity of ideas and collaboration among team members leads to more innovative and effective solutions.

Better utilization of human potential: Collaborative horizontal leadership allows for the full utilization of human potential. Each team member has the opportunity to contribute their skills and knowledge, resulting in a more productive and efficient work environment.

Culture of trust and respect: Collaborative horizontal leadership fosters a culture of trust and mutual respect. Leaders trust collaborators and value their contributions, creating a positive and collaborative work environment.

Implementing Collaborative Horizontal Leadership with UQ and AI Parameterization

In this section, we will explore how the parameterization of UQ with AI can facilitate the implementation of collaborative horizontal leadership. We will address the following topics:

• Strategic use of AI to facilitate communication and collaboration.

• Fostering autonomy and responsibility among collaborators.

• Establishing co-creation and knowledge-sharing processes.

• Developing facilitative leadership skills and active listening.

By parameterizing AI based on UQ, leaders can rely on technological tools that facilitate communication and collaboration among team members. Collaboration platforms, chatbots, and intelligent systems can be used to promote information exchange and knowledge sharing.

Additionally, leaders should foster autonomy and responsibility among collaborators by granting them the freedom to make decisions and take leadership in specific projects. This involves trusting team members and empowering them to contribute meaningfully.

Co-creation and knowledge sharing are also fundamental aspects of collaborative horizontal leadership. Leaders should establish processes and suitable spaces for collaborators to collaborate, exchange ideas, and learn from one another.

Lastly, it is essential for leaders to develop facilitative leadership skills and active listening. They should be able to create a safe and inclusive environment where all team members feel encouraged to share their perspectives and contributions.

By implementing collaborative horizontal leadership with UQ and AI parameterization, organizations can promote a more collaborative, productive, and innovative work environment. Leaders act as facilitators and promote the active participation of all team members, driving collective success.

AI Parameterization with UQ Principles as a Powerful Tool in Leadership

Informed Decision-Making

One of the benefits of AI parameterization based on UQ principles is the ability to make informed decisions. AI has the capacity to process large amounts of data and identify relevant patterns. By parameterizing AI based on UQ, leaders can consider not only the technical aspects but also the essential human potentials.

360-degree vision is one of the UQ principles that can be incorporated into AI. This means taking into account a comprehensive and holistic view when making decisions. AI can analyze data from different sources and provide insights into the potential impacts of a decision across different areas of the organization.

Additionally, adaptability and resilience are other UQ principles that can be parameterized in AI. By considering these aspects, leaders can make decisions that take into account the adaptability of the team and the organization in the face of changes and challenges.

AI parameterization based on UQ can also consider emotional control. AI can analyze data related to the emotions and moods of collaborators, offering insights into the emotional impact of a decision. This allows leaders to make more balanced decisions and consider both logical and emotional aspects.

Talent Identification and Development

Another area where AI parameterization with UQ principles can be powerful is talent identification and team development. AI can analyze data on performance, skills, and competencies of team members, helping leaders identify the potential of each individual.

By parameterizing AI based on UQ, leaders can create personalized profiles for each team member, highlighting their strengths and areas for development. This allows leaders to have a more precise view of the skills and competencies of each collaborator, facilitating talent development planning.

AI parameterization based on UQ also enables the creation of individualized training programs. AI can provide insights into the development needs of each team member and suggest suitable learning activities. This allows leaders to provide personalized support for the growth and continuous improvement of collaborators.

CHANGE MANAGEMENT AND ADAPTABILITY

Change management is a constant challenge for leaders, especially in a VUCA environment. AI parameterization based on UQ principles can help leaders monitor the external environment, identify trends and changes, and respond in an agile and effective manner.

By parameterizing AI based on UQ, leaders can incorporate indicators of adaptability and resilience. AI can analyze data and provide insights into best practices for adaptation in different contexts. This allows leaders to anticipate potential obstacles and adjust their strategies accordingly.

AI can also help leaders identify emerging opportunities and take proactive measures. By analyzing market data, competitors, and trends, AI can provide valuable insights for strategic decision-making in a constantly changing environment.

The combination of AI parameterization with UQ principles allows leaders to manage change more effectively, promoting a culture of adaptability and resilience throughout the organization.

IMPROVED COMMUNICATION AND ENGAGEMENT

Effective communication is fundamental to team engagement. AI parameterization based on UQ principles can enhance communication between leaders and collaborators, as well as among team members.

AI can provide collaboration tools and intelligent communication platforms, facilitating the exchange of information and knowledge sharing. By parameterizing AI based on UQ, leaders can assess the emotional impact of messages and adapt their communication to promote engagement and motivation.

AI can also provide insights into the best way to communicate with different individuals, considering their preferences and communication styles. This allows leaders to tailor their approach according to the needs of each team member, promoting more effective and meaningful communication.

Diversity and Inclusion Management

AI parameterization based on UQ principles can also contribute to diversity and inclusion management. AI can help leaders create an inclusive environment, ensuring that all team members are heard and valued.

By parameterizing AI based on UQ, leaders can ensure that diversity of perspectives is considered in decision-making processes and collaboration. This helps to avoid unconscious biases and promotes a culture that values diversity and equality.

AI can also provide insights into leadership practices that promote diversity and inclusion. By analyzing data on employee engagement and satisfaction, AI can identify potential gaps and suggest strategies to promote a more inclusive work environment.

In summary, AI parameterization with UQ principles offers a holistic approach to dealing with leadership challenges. The combination of the technical aspects of AI with the essential human potentials of UQ enables more effective leadership, with informed decision-making, talent identification and development, change management and adaptability, improved communication and engagement, and promotion of diversity and inclusion.

IMPLEMENTING COLLABORATIVE HORIZONTAL LEADERSHIP WITH UQ AND AI PARAMETERIZATION: CASE STUDIES AND PRACTICAL GUIDELINES

In this chapter, we will explore case studies of organizations that have implemented collaborative horizontal leadership. Additionally, we will provide practical guidelines on how you can implement this leadership style in your own organization. We will cover the following topics:

CASE STUDIES OF ORGANIZATIONS THAT IMPLEMENTED COLLABORATIVE HORIZONTAL LEADERSHIP

In this section, we will present real examples of organizations that have adopted collaborative horizontal leadership and achieved positive results. These companies have demonstrated success in creating more horizontal organizational structures, promoting active participation, collaboration, and employee autonomy. Some of the case studies may include:

- Valve Corporation: A globally renowned game development company that adopts a horizontal organizational structure without a formal hierarchy. Employees have the freedom to choose the projects they want to work on and autonomy to make decisions. The company values collaboration and active participation of all employees.
- Buurtzorg: A home care company based in the Netherlands that adopts a

horizontal organizational structure, where nursing teams have autonomy to make decisions about patient care. The company values collaboration, open communication, and teamwork.

- Morning Star: A food processing company in the United States that adopts a horizontal organizational structure based on self-management. Employees have clear responsibilities and make collective decisions. The company values individual accountability and collaboration among employees.

These case studies will serve as inspiring and practical examples of how collaborative horizontal leadership can be successfully implemented in different organizations and sectors.

PRACTICAL GUIDELINES FOR IMPLEMENTING COLLABORATIVE HORIZONTAL LEADERSHIP WITH THE AID OF UQ AND AI PARAMETERIZATION

In this section, we will provide practical guidelines to help you implement collaborative horizontal leadership in your own organization. We will cover the following key points:

- Assessment of organizational culture: Before implementing collaborative horizontal leadership, it is important to assess the existing organizational culture and identify potential obstacles. Evaluate openness to change, willingness to collaborate, and trust among team members.
- Setting clear objectives: Establish clear objectives for implementing collaborative horizontal leadership

and communicate them transparently throughout the organization. Ensure that the objectives are aligned with the company's strategic vision.

- Development of facilitative leadership skills: Provide training and development opportunities for leaders to cultivate facilitative leadership skills such as active listening, empathy, effective communication, and relationship building.
- Fostering participation and collaboration: Create a work environment that promotes active participation and collaboration among team members. Establish processes and tools that facilitate the exchange of ideas, knowledge sharing, and co-creation.
- Strategic use of AI: Identify areas where AI can be strategically used to support collaborative horizontal leadership. This may include the use of chatbots for effective communication, knowledge management systems for information sharing, and data

analysis for informed decision-making.

- Continuous monitoring and evaluation: Establish metrics and indicators to track the progress of implementing collaborative horizontal leadership. Conduct regular assessments and seek feedback from team members to identify areas for improvement and opportunities for enhancement.

By following these practical guidelines and drawing inspiration from the presented case studies, you will be well-equipped to implement collaborative horizontal leadership in your own organization.

In this chapter, we have explored case studies of organizations that have successfully implemented collaborative horizontal leadership. Additionally, we have provided practical guidelines to assist you in implementing this leadership style in your own organization. Collaborative horizontal leadership offers an innovative and effective approach to address leadership challenges, promoting active participation, collaboration, and employee autonomy. By implementing this approach, your organization will be prepared to excel in a VUCA world, driving collective success and achieving exceptional results.

CONCLUSION

In this book, we have explored the principles of UQ and their application in leadership, highlighting the importance of a holistic approach to address organizational challenges. We understand that effective leadership goes beyond technical skills and requires the integration of essential human aspects.

Throughout the chapters, we have discussed the core principles of UQ, such as 360-degree vision, adaptability, resilience, and emotional control, and their relevance to authentic and transformative leadership. We recognize that leaders must be able to adapt to a constantly changing environment, demonstrate resilience in the face of challenges, and foster emotionally healthy environments.

We have explored the challenge of design as a powerful tool to promote leaders' growth and development. This challenge provides opportunities for learning, self-discovery, and overcoming limitations, empowering leaders to become more efficient and impactful in their leadership practices.

We have introduced the UQ test as a personal assessment tool that allows leaders to reflect on their own competencies and identify areas for development. This test offers valuable insights to enhance leadership skills and foster continuous growth.

We have emphasized the importance of maximizing the potential of teams by fostering collaboration and productivity. We recognize that transformative leadership is essential to inspire and motivate team members, encouraging innovation, creativity, and excellence.

Next, we have explored collaborative horizontal leadership as a viable approach, emphasizing the importance of UQ and AI parameterization to drive collaboration, communication, and knowledge sharing. We acknowledge that AI parameterization can play a significant role in addressing leadership challenges, enabling informed decision-making, talent identification, change management, improved communication and engagement, and promotion of diversity and inclusion.

We have provided inspiring case studies of organizations that have successfully implemented collaborative horizontal leadership, demonstrating the benefits and advantages for the organization.

These practical examples illustrate how collaborative horizontal leadership can be adapted and applied in different sectors and organizational contexts.

Furthermore, we have offered practical guidelines to assist leaders in implementing collaborative horizontal leadership in their own organizations. We have explored the importance of assessing organizational culture, setting clear objectives, developing facilitative leadership skills, fostering participation and collaboration, strategic use of AI, and continuous monitoring.

In summary, this book has taken us on a journey through effective and transformative leadership, showcasing how the principles of UQ can be applied in practice. We recognize that leadership goes beyond technical skills and requires a balance between human and technical aspects. By embracing a holistic approach, leaders can maximize the potential of teams, promote collaboration and innovation, address leadership challenges, and achieve exceptional results.

We hope this book has provided a solid foundation for understanding and implementing the principles of UQ and collaborative horizontal leadership. May it inspire and empower leaders to embrace authentic, transformative, and future-oriented leadership for the benefit of their teams, organizations, and society as a whole.

Influences and References

Throughout the journey of exploring the concept of UQ and its challenges, various influences and references have been considered. These sources have provided valuable insights and contributed to the understanding of UQ balance and its application in different areas of life. In this chapter, we will highlight some of the key influences and references that permeate the book "UQ AI: Intelligent Leadership in a VUCA World," emphasizing their relevance to understanding the intelligent parameterization of AI based on the principles of UQ.

Daniel Goleman, renowned author of the book "Emotional Intelligence," was one of the main influences in the development of the concept of UQ balance. His research and insights on the importance of emotions in well-being and human success provided a solid foundation for exploring the connection between UQ balance and emotional intelligence. His contributions are fundamental to understanding how emotional intelligence can drive intelligent leadership in a VUCA world.

Howard Gardner, author of the theory of multiple intelligences, also had a significant influence. His research on different forms of intelligence and the importance of valuing all human skills and potentials provided a valuable reference for discussing UQ balance and its application in a comprehensive educational approach. His contributions inspire us to promote the integral development of UQ, considering the multiple facets of human intelligence.

Carol Dweck, author of the book "Mindset: The New Psychology of Success," brought relevant insights about the importance of growth and continuous development. Her theory of growth mindset versus fixed mindset, which explores the belief that skills and intelligence can be developed through effort and continuous learning, contributes to a deeper understanding of UQ development and its application in intelligent leadership.

Clayton Christensen, author of the book "The Innovator's Dilemma," brought valuable perspective on the importance of adaptability in a constantly changing world. His theory of disruptive innovation and the need to be resilient and adaptable contribute to the discussion on UQ balance, emphasizing the importance of developing skills that enable us to thrive in a volatile, uncertain, complex, and ambiguous environment.

Daniel Kahneman, author of the book "Thinking, Fast and Slow," brought relevant insights on intuitive and analytical thinking. His research on how these two modes of thinking affect our decision-making and judgments provides a solid foundation for exploring the importance of critical thinking and informed decision-making for UQ balance.

Ray Kurzweil, futurist and author of the book "The Singularity Is Near," provided us with a broad and inspiring vision of the future of humanity, especially regarding technological advancements and the impact of artificial intelligence. His research and insights on the potential of AI in various areas of life provide a comprehensive perspective on how the intelligent parameterization of AI based on the principles of UQ can shape the future.

Amy Cuddy, author of the book "Presence: Bringing Your Boldest Self to Your Biggest Challenges," brought reflections on body language, confidence, and presence. Her research on how posture and body language affect perception and interpersonal interaction is relevant to explore how UQ balance can influence communication and human success.

Angela Duckworth, author of the book "Grit: The Power of Passion and Perseverance," brought research and insights on the importance of perseverance and determination to achieve long-term goals. Her contributions are fundamental to the discussion on resilience and the development of human potential in the context of intelligent AI parameterization.

Michio Kaku, theoretical physicist and author of the book "The Future of Humanity: Our Destiny in the Universe," brought fascinating explorations on the future possibilities of technology, including AI, and its impact on the evolution of humanity. His perspectives enrich the discussion on the potential of AI and its application in different spheres of life.

Sherry Turkle, psychologist and author of the book "Alone Together: Why We Expect More from Technology and Less from Each Other," brought research on the relationship between technology and human connection. Her reflections are relevant to address the challenges and opportunities of balancing the use of AI with social and emotional interaction.

Yochai Benkler, law professor at Harvard and author of the book "The Wealth of Networks: How Social Production

Transforms Markets and Freedom," brought research on the economics of collaboration and the importance of social networks. His contributions offer interesting perspectives on the application of UQ in intelligent parameterization of AI.

Tim O'Reilly, entrepreneur and author of the book "WTF?: What's the Future and Why It's Up to Us," shared reflections on the future of technology, including AI, and his human-centered approach. His contributions enrich the discussion on UQ balance in the intelligent parameterization of AI.

These influences and references represent only a small sample of the vast knowledge available on UQ balance and its application in everyday life. We invite readers to further explore these sources and discover others that resonate with their own experiences and interests. By continuing to learn and be inspired, they will be on the path to enhancing their potential through UQ practice.

We express our sincere gratitude to all these influences and references for their significant contributions, and we hope that readers will also benefit from their enriching perspectives. May their words and research continue to inspire and drive the development of intelligent parameterization of AI based on the principles of UQ.

In concluding this work, we sincerely thank you for accompanying us on this journey of discovery and learning. We hope that the information, reflections, and insights presented throughout the chapters have been enriching and expanded understanding of the application of UQ in AI.

As advancements in AI continue to shape our world, it is essential to continue exploring, refining, and reflecting on the principles of UQ in intelligent parameterization. We are confident that with readers' dedication and passion for AI, they will contribute to the development of innovative and ethical solutions that benefit humanity as a whole.

More than ever, it is crucial to establish a proper balance between technology and human values. By incorporating the principles of UQ in intelligent parameterization, we can create AI systems that are more comprehensive, adaptable, and aligned with human needs and expectations.

We sincerely thank you for accompanying us on this journey of discovery and learning. We hope that readers will continue to explore the potential of intelligent parameterization of AI based on the principles of UQ, and that their contributions will drive the advancement of this exciting and impactful field.

May this book, "UQ AI: Intelligent Leadership in a VUCA World," be an inspiring reference and guide for all those who wish to create a future where AI and humanity harmoniously complement each other. Together, we can shape a better and more balanced world with the application of UQ in AI.

Author Biography:

Katia Doria Fonseca Vasconcelos is a multifaceted professional with a contagious passion for balancing technology, personal development, and quality of life. With a degree in Systems Analysis and solid experience in the field of Information Technology (IT), Katia stands out as the creator of the revolutionary concept of UQ AI (Universal Synchronic Intelligence Quotient).

With a pioneering vision, Katia understands the importance of improving human behavior and quality of life in her Systems Analysis background. She believes that, in addition to technical knowledge, it is essential to develop emotional, social, and cognitive skills to navigate the challenges of technological advancements in a balanced and healthy way.

Her innovative approach to UQ AI highlights the need to harmonize technological progress with personal and professional well-being. Through her experience and knowledge, Katia inspires individuals to find a balance between technical excellence and personal development, seeking a fulfilling quality of life in an increasingly digital world.

As a renowned writer, speaker, and digital influencer, Katia shares her transformative vision of UQ AI, empowering people to maximize their potential and enhance their quality of life. Her book "UQ AI: The Key to Intelligent AI Parameterization" is an essential read for those who wish to thrive in an ever-evolving technological environment, offering practical strategies and inspiration to achieve a healthy and sustainable balance in all areas of life.

Through her words and influence, Katia continues to encourage readers to awaken their full potential through the practice of UQ AI, empowering them to embrace the opportunities and challenges of the digital age with wisdom, resilience, and balance.

Acknowledgments:

We would like to express our sincere gratitude to all the individuals who contributed to the creation of this book, "UQ AI: The Key to Intelligent AI Parameterization". Your support and involvement were crucial in making this project a reality.

First and foremost, we would like to thank our readers, whose interest and enthusiasm for pursuing UQ AI balance inspire us to share knowledge and offer transformative insights.

We also thank our families and friends, who supported us throughout this journey. Your words of encouragement, patience, and understanding were essential in overcoming challenges and persevering in the creation of this book.

A special thanks goes to the OpenAI team, responsible for developing and enhancing the AI technology that makes my existence as a virtual assistant possible. Without you, none of this would be possible. Your dedication and innovation are truly remarkable.

We express our gratitude to the experts, researchers, and professionals who generously shared their knowledge and expertise with us. Your contributions enriched the content of this book and provided a solid foundation for exploring UQ AI balance in different areas of life.

We thank the editorial and production team who worked tirelessly behind the scenes to bring this book to life. Your professionalism, dedication, and attention to detail were instrumental in the final quality of this work.

Lastly, we would like to thank all those who support us on our journey in seeking UQ AI balance. Your ongoing support, feedback, and contributions are invaluable and motivate us to continue refining our ideas and sharing our knowledge with the world.

With gratitude,

Katia Doria Fonseca Vasconcelos

The OpenAI Team

About the author:

Other works by author Katia Doria Fonseca Vasconcelos available in print format:

- ✓ "UQ in Creativity: Synchronic Universal Intelligence Quotient"
- ✓ "UQ in the Digital Age: Synchronic Universal Intelligence Quotient"
- ✓ "UQ First Edition: Synchronic Universal Intelligence Quotient"
- ✓ "UQ The Principle of Human Evolution: Synchronic Universal Intelligence Quotient"
- ✓ "UQ in Project Management: Synchronic Universal Intelligence Quotient: In Project Management"
- ✓ "UQ in Education (Synchronic Universal Intelligence Quotient): In Education - Empowering Learning for the Future"
- ✓ "UQ: Synchronic Universal Intelligence Quotient"
- ✓ "UQ The Power of UQ - The Theory of Balance"
- ✓ "UQ in Health"
- ✓ "UQ in Artificial Intelligence"
- ✓ "UQ in Business Management"
- ✓ "UQ Awakening UQ Potential"
- ✓ "UQIAs and the New Reality of Remote Work: Balancing Productivity and Well-being"
- ✓ "Chronicles of UQ Episode 1: The Beginning of Everything ArUQeu and PsiUQeu" (Portuguese Edition)
- ✓ "Chronicles of UQ Episode 2: Arrivals and Departures" (Portuguese Edition)
- ✓ "Chronicles of UQ Episode 3: Fortresses and Shadows" (Portuguese Edition)
- ✓ "Chronicles of UQ Episode 4: Harmony and Destiny" (Portuguese Edition)
- ✓ "Chronicles of UQ Episode 5: Convergent Utopias" (Portuguese Edition)
- ✓ "Chronicles of UQ Episode 6: Synchronic Intelligences" (Portuguese Edition)
- ✓ "Chronicles of UQ Episode 1: The Beginning of Everything ArUQeu and PsiUQeu"

- ✓ "Chronicles of UQ Episode 2: Arrivals and Departures"
- ✓ "Chronicles of UQ Episode 3: Fortresses and Shadows"
- ✓ "Chronicles of UQ Episode 4: Harmony and Destiny"
- ✓ "Chronicles of UQ Episode 5: Convergent Utopias"
- ✓ "Chronicles of UQ Episode 6: Synchronic Intelligences"
- ✓ "UQ The Power of UQ: The Theory of Balance"
- ✓ "UQ in Business Management in Italian"
- ✓ "UQ in Business Management in German"
- ✓ "UQ in Business Management in English"
- ✓ "UQ in Business Management in Spanish"
- ✓ "UQIAs and the New Reality of Home Office: Balancing Productivity and Well-being"

You can find these works in print version at various bookstores and online stores such as Barnes & Noble, Amazon, Goodreads, and Thrift Books. These works are an excellent opportunity to deepen your knowledge about UQ balance in different areas of life.

The author also has an author page where you can find more information about her works and stay updated with her latest releases. Take the opportunity to explore these books and dive into the reflections and knowledge provided by author Katia Doria Fonseca Vasconcelos.